ANIMALS AND THEIR HABITATS
Mountains and Polar Regions

WORLD
BOOK

A Scott Fetzer company
Chicago

www.worldbookonline.com

World Book, Inc.
233 N. Michigan Avenue
Chicago, IL 60601
U.S.A.

For information about other World Book publications,
visit our website at http://www.worldbookonline.com
or call 1-800-WORLDBK (967-5325).

For information about sales to schools and libraries, call
1-800-975-3250 (United States), or 1-800-837-5365 (Canada).

Staff

Executive Committee
President: Donald D. Keller
Vice President and Editor in Chief: Paul A. Kobasa
Vice President, Marketing/Digital Products: Sean Klunder
Vice President, International: Richard Flower
Controller: Yan Chen
Director, Human Resources: Bev Ecker

Editorial

Associate Director, Supplementary Publications:
 Scott Thomas
Managing Editor, Supplementary Publications:
 Barbara A. Mayes
Associate Manager, Supplementary Publications:
 Cassie Mayer
Editors: Brian Johnson and Kristina Vaicikonis
Researcher: Annie Brodsky
Editorial Assistant: Ethel Matthews
Manager, Contracts & Compliance
 (Rights & Permissions): Loranne K. Shields
Indexer: David Pofelski
Writer: David Alderton
Project Editor: Sarah Uttridge
Editorial Assistant: Kieron Connolly
Design: Andrew Easton

Graphics and Design

Senior Manager: Tom Evans
Senior Designer: Don Di Sante
Manager, Cartography: Wayne K. Pichler
Senior Cartographer: John Rejba

Pre-Press and Manufacturing

Director: Carma Fazio
Manufacturing Manager: Steven K. Hueppchen
Senior Production Manager: Janice Rossing
Production/Technology Manager: Anne Fritzinger
Proofreader: Emilie Schrage

Library of Congress Cataloging-in-Publication Data
Mountains and polar regions.
    p. cm. -- (Animals and their habitats)
    Summary: "Text and illustrations introduce several
animal species that live in mountain ranges and polar
regions. Detailed captions describe each animal, while
inset maps show where the animals can be found
around the world. Special features include a glossary, a
climate zone map, photographs, and an index." --
Provided by publisher.
    Includes index.
    ISBN 978-0-7166-0448-8
    1. Mountain animals--Juvenile literature. 2. Animals--
Polar regions--Juvenile literature. I. World Book, Inc.
QL113.M686 2012
591.75'3--dc23
                                        2012005837

Animals and Their Habitats
Set ISBN: 978-0-7166-0441-9

Printed in China by Leo Paper Products LTD.,
Heshan, Guangdong
1st printing July 2012

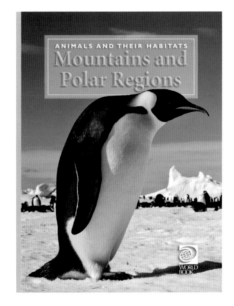

The emperor penguin is the largest of
all penguins. Like other polar animals
and animals that live on mountains,
emperor penguins are well adapted to
life under harsh conditions, especially
frigid temperatures.

© Photo Researchers (J.-L. Klein and
M.-L. Hubert)

Contents

Introduction

Mountain ranges are some of the most stunning landscapes on our planet. They rise majestically from the plains, soaring into the thin, cold air. Some mountain ranges span entire continents. Mountains can also be forbidding. The terrain is rugged, and the temperature falls with increasing elevation. As a result, tall mountains may be permanently capped with snow and ice, even when they are surrounded by desert. Mountains support a rich variety of animal life. Different animals live at different elevations. Some migrate up and down the mountain with the changing seasons.

Many kinds of goats and antelopes live on mountain slopes. Their sharp hoofs enable them to climb steep rock faces. Yaks live in the icy mountains of central Asia. They are protected from the cold by shaggy fur and fat. Rodents and even some kinds of amphibians live on mountains. Large *predators* (hunting animals), including snow leopards and wolves, are also found on many mountains.

Polar regions have some of the harshest conditions on our planet. There are two polar regions. The Arctic surrounds the North Pole, and the Antarctic surrounds the South Pole. Winters are especially difficult in polar regions. During the winter, the sun does not appear for weeks and temperatures rank as the coldest on Earth. Scientists recorded a low temperature of −128.6 °F (−89.2 °C) in Antarctica. Violent storms with winds that reach up to 125 miles (200 kilometers) per hour make the air seem even colder. Very few animals can survive in this challenging *habitat* (the type of place in which an animal lives).

YAK

SOUTHERN ELEPHANT SEAL

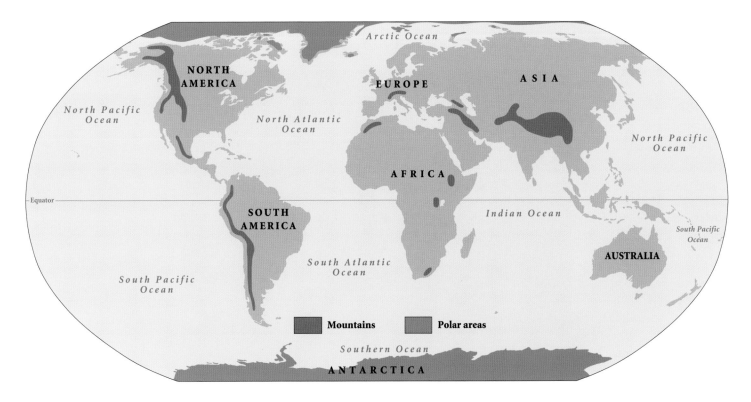

MOUNTAINS AND POLAR REGIONS

GOLDEN EAGLE

Animals that live in polar regions have *adaptations* (characteristics) that protect them from the cold. Many have layers of *blubber* (fat) under the skin. Polar animals also tend to be large, which helps them hold in body heat. For example, a male southern elephant seal may weigh as much as 8,800 pounds (4,000 kilograms).

Many polar animals live and hunt in the sea, because there is little food available on land. But the land also has relatively few predators, which offers advantages to some animals. For example, the emperor penguin is the only large animal to spend the winter on the surface of Antarctica. The penguins brave low temperatures and violent storms because there are no predators to attack them as they *incubate* (sit on) their eggs. The penguins survive by huddling together in large groups to share their body heat. Every penguin takes its turn at the edge of the huddle, where it is coldest.

Bezoar Ibex

This species is considered the original ancestor of the *domesticated* (tamed) goat. The domestication of the ibex began between 8,000 and 9,000 years ago in southwestern Asia.

VITAL STATISTICS

WEIGHT	154–176 lb (70–80 kg); females are lighter than males
LENGTH	4–5 ft (1.2–1.6 cm)
SEXUAL MATURITY	Females 1.5–2.5 years; males 3.5–4 years
LENGTH OF PREGNANCY	About 160 days
NUMBER OF OFFSPRING	Normally 1 kid, but occasionally 2
DIET	Browses on a wide range of vegetation
LIFE SPAN	Around 12 years in the wild; can be up to 22 in captivity

WHERE IN THE WORLD?

Western Asia, occurring in the Anatolian region of Turkey as well as in northeastern Iraq, Iran, western Afghanistan, the eastern Caucasus, and far south Turkmenistan.

ANIMAL FACTS

These animals live at relatively high altitudes, on craggy cliffs and upland pastures. They sometimes gather in large herds numbering up to 500, though more typical groups consist of 5 to 20 individuals. Mating occurs from fall through to midwinter. At this stage, males become far more aggressive toward each other, battling with their horns. Herds are also likely to move down to lower levels during the winter, as food may be easier to find there.

Bezoar ibexes can jump, too.

HORNS
Males have long, curved horns, measuring up to 65 inches (165 centimeters). A female's horns are shorter.

COAT
The reddish-brown coat turns brownish-gray in the winter among mature males.

BEARD
Mature males have a very distinctive long, black beard on the chin.

CALLUSES
These hardened areas of skin form on the knees because the animal rests on them.

THE HIGH LIFE
Bezoar ibexes use their climbing skills to reach and browse on leaves and shoots growing well off the ground.

HOW BIG IS IT?

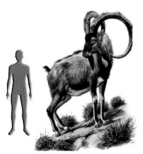

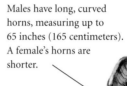

Alpine Ibex

VITAL STATISTICS

WEIGHT	88–265 lb (40–120 kg); males can be twice as heavy as females
LENGTH	3–6.5 ft (0.9–2 m), including tail
SEXUAL MATURITY	Females breed from 1 year; males from 2 years
LENGTH OF PREGNANCY	Typically 165–170 days
NUMBER OF OFFSPRING	Usually 1 kid, occasionally 2
DIET	Eats grass, flowers, moss, leaves, and twigs
LIFE SPAN	10–14 years

ANIMAL FACTS

This species is able to climb steep mountain slopes, where few *predators* (hunting animals) can follow. Alpine ibexes often seek out southern-facing slopes at lower altitudes during the winter, where food is easier to find. In the winter, herds of females are joined by males. The sexes live separately for the rest of the year.

Going down safely

Climbing up

Alpine ibexes can jump well, even when they are as young as two days old. This ability helps to ensure their survival in mountainous terrain.

WHERE IN THE WORLD?

Lives in the European Alps, from the border area between France and Italy, east through Switzerland to Austria, at altitudes of 5,100 to 10,200 feet (1,600 to 3,200 meters).

PLAYFUL FIGHTING
Males will often rear up and joust with their horns.

HORNS
The male has ridges on the horns, which can reach up to 40 inches (100 centimeters) long.

COAT
Males over 7 years old develop a dark chestnut-brown winter coat.

JUMPING STRENGTH
The strength of these ibexes lies in the muscular power of their hind legs.

HOW BIG IS IT?

Himalayan Tahr

VITAL STATISTICS

WEIGHT	More than 220 lb (99.7 kg)
LENGTH	About 5.5 ft (1.7 m), including tail
SEXUAL MATURITY	2–3 years; mating occurs from October to January
LENGTH OF PREGNANCY	About 217 days
NUMBER OF OFFSPRING	A single youngster, occasionally 2; weaned by 6 months
DIET	Eats grasses, leaves, and flowers
LIFE SPAN	Up to 10 years in the wild, but can be over 20 in captivity

This goatlike antelope lives on the rugged slopes of the Himalaya mountain range. It is most likely to be encountered in wooded areas.

WHERE IN THE WORLD?

Lives in the wild in Asia, in the vicinity of the Himalaya mountains, extending from Kashmir to Sikkim. It has also been introduced to New Zealand.

ANIMAL FACTS

Himalayan tahrs live in herds that typically have about 15 individuals. But old males may live on their own, probably after being driven out by younger rivals. Males fight for dominance, wrestling with their horns in a trial of strength. Tahrs are very alert and disappear at any hint of danger, jumping over rough terrain without difficulty.

Male

Female

HORNS
Present in both sexes, the horns are triangular and curve inward at their tips, growing up to 18 inches (45 centimeters) long.

EARS
Like most animals that live in cold environments, the Himalayan tahr has small ears, to reduce the risk of frostbite.

MANE
The mane is a distinctive feature of males during the winter, when the coat is thicker.

LEGS
The legs are quite short and stocky.

HOW BIG IS IT?

DAILY ROUTINE
During the middle of the day, Himalayan tahrs rest among rocks, preferring to seek food in the morning and evening.

Mountain Goat

VITAL STATISTICS

WEIGHT	100–300 lb (45–136 kg)
LENGTH	5–5.5 ft (1.5–1.6 m), including tail
SEXUAL MATURITY	About 1.5 years
LENGTH OF PREGNANCY	175–180 days
NUMBER OF OFFSPRING	Normally 1 kid, although 2 or 3 have been recorded
DIET	Grazes on grass and lichens, and also browses on taller plants
LIFE SPAN	Females up to 18 years; males up to 14 years

ANIMAL FACTS

The lives of these goats are influenced by the changing seasons. During the summer, they live in small groups or wander individually. In winter, they form larger herds. Mating takes place at this time, with the young born during the early summer, when weather conditions are more favorable. Conflict is most likely to arise between males during the breeding season. Instead of battling head-on, they may gore their opponent's flanks, inflicting serious or even deadly wounds.

The feet have special stopper pads, for greater control.

Unlike many other mountain animals, mountain goats remain at high elevations all year long, even in the winter. Few animals can match their speed and grace on difficult mountain terrain.

WHERE IN THE WORLD?

Southern Alaska and northwestern Canada, south to Utah and Colorado, through the Rocky Mountains. Introduced in some areas.

TAIL
The tail is short and bushy and covered with fur.

COAT
Long, soft fur provides excellent insulation and creates a ridge running along the back. The coat becomes thicker in the winter.

HORNS
Horns are curved and present in both sexes, growing to a similar length of 8 to 10 inches (20 to 25 centimeters).

COLORATION
During the summer the coat is white, but it becomes more yellow in winter.

HOW BIG IS IT?

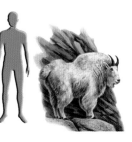

HEAD FOR HEIGHTS
These goats maintain a secure footing on wet or icy cliff faces thanks in part to the hard, sharp edges of their hoofs.

Chamois (Gemse)

VITAL STATISTICS

WEIGHT	About 80 lb (36 kg)
LENGTH	4–4.75 ft (1.2–1.4 m), including tail
SEXUAL MATURITY	Females about 2.5 years; males 3.5–4 years
LENGTH OF PREGNANCY	About 170 days; young are weaned by about 6 months
NUMBER OF OFFSPRING	1, occasionally 2 or 3
DIET	Grazes on grass; also browses on taller plants
LIFE SPAN	Typically around 14 years, but can live up to 22

These agile mountain goats have been hunted extensively for their hides, which are manufactured into chamois leather used for polishing cars and glass.

WHERE IN THE WORLD?

Lives in the mountainous regions of central and southern Europe, notably in the Alps and Carpathians, extending through parts of Asia Minor to the Caucasus.

ANIMAL FACTS

In the summer, herds of chamois graze on the plants in *alpine* (mountain) meadows. In the winter, food is harder to find, even at lower altitudes. Chamois will eat shoots of pines and have been known to survive without feeding at all for two weeks. Such *predators* (hunting animals) as bears and wolves hunt chamois, especially the young.

Summer coat

Winter coat

COAT
This varies in appearance throughout the year. It is shorter and lighter both in weight and color during the summer.

HORNS
The horns measure up to 8 inches (20 centimeters) long and occur in both sexes. They are slender, curling over at their tips.

HOOFS
Chamois have slightly elastic pads on their hoofs, which act as shock absorbers, helping them to maintain their balance.

HOW BIG IS IT?

FOSTER PARENTS
If a female chamois dies, other herd members will look after her offspring. Deaths are most common during winter.

Yak

VITAL STATISTICS

WEIGHT	1,100-1,200 lb (499-544 kg)
LENGTH	Up to 12.5 ft (3.8 m), including tail; reaches 6.5 ft (2 m) tall at the shoulder
SEXUAL MATURITY	6 years
LENGTH OF PREGNANCY	About 258 days; calves weaned by about 1 year old
NUMBER OF OFFSPRING	1 calf every second year
DIET	Grazes on grass; also eats other plants and tubers
LIFE SPAN	Up to 23 years

ANIMAL FACTS

The domestication of the yak began over 10,000 years ago. Today, this species is very important to the people of central Asia. Compared with the wild yak, domesticated yaks are smaller in size and their coats have a wider variety of colors. Few animals are as hardy. Yaks can be found in areas where the temperature drops far below freezing in winter. In fact, their thick coats can be uncomfortable in hot weather. Yaks mate in September. The bulls fight over the cows.

The wild yak is now scarce, with fewer than about 15,000 individuals remaining. However, people keep millions of *domesticated* (tamed) yak, raising them for their milk, meat, and wool.

WHERE IN THE WORLD?

Lives at altitudes of 12,800 to 19,200 feet (4,000 to 6,000 meters) in Tibet. Also found in China, India, and possibly Nepal.

HORNS
Horns curve upward, growing up to 38 inches (95 centimeters) long in males, shorter in females.

HEAD AND SHOULDERS
The head is relatively low-set, and the shoulders have a distinctive humped appearance.

LEGS AND FEET
Yaks have short legs and large hoofs, with *dewclaws* (extra claws) to prevent them from slipping.

COAT
The coat is usually blackish-brown. A few wild yaks with golden coats have been seen.

BATTLING ON THE PLATEAU
Two bulls clash during the breeding season. Wild yaks emit distinctive grunting calls during this time of year. Domestic yaks grunt throughout the year.

HOW BIG IS IT?

Wild yak (left) and domesticated yak (right).

Vicuña

Vicuñas are the smallest member of the camel family. Their coats have long been prized for their very soft wool. They usually live in herds made up of one male and several females and their offspring.

VITAL STATISTICS

WEIGHT	75–140 lb (35–65 kg); males are heavier
LENGTH	5.3–6 ft (1.6–1.8 m), including tail; up to 3.1 ft (0.9 m) tall
SEXUAL MATURITY	About 24 months
LENGTH OF PREGNANCY	330–350 days; weaned 6–8 months later
NUMBER OF OFFSPRING	1
DIET	Feeds mainly on grass, which inflicts heavy wear on the teeth
LIFE SPAN	20 years in the wild; up to 25 in captivity

ANIMAL FACTS

Vicuñas are vulnerable to attacks by mountain lions. The young are also at risk from foxes. As a result, vicuñas are constantly alert to danger, communicating with other members of the herd by means of a shrill whistle. They live high in the mountains, where the air is thin. Nevertheless, they can run at speeds of up to 30 miles (50 kilometers) per hour. Their hearts are enlarged to pump their thick blood around the body.

The young are ultimately driven from the herd by the resident male.

WHERE IN THE WORLD?

Lives in western South America at altitudes of 11,700 to 19,300 feet (3,500 to 5,800 meters) in the Andean mountain regions of Argentina, Bolivia, Chile, and Peru.

HEAD
The head is small and wedge-shaped; the ears are triangular.

TEETH
The vicuña is unusual among hooved animals in having *incisor* (cutting) teeth that grow throughout its life.

MANE
The mane on the chest is made of hairs up to 12 inches (30 centimeters) long.

COLORATION
The coat is light brown above, with white areas on the belly and legs.

COAT
By the 1960's, so many vicuñas had been killed for their wool that the animal was endangered. Since then, conservation efforts have increased vicuña populations.

DAILY ROUTINE
During the day, the herd comes down from the hills to feed on grasses and other vegetation. As dusk falls, the herd returns to the hills to sleep.

HOW BIG IS IT?

Llama

SPECIES • *Lama glama*

People have raised llamas for thousands of years. Llamas have been important pack animals, carrying burdens on paths high in the mountains. They also provide valuable wool.

VITAL STATISTICS

WEIGHT	250 lb (113 kg)
LENGTH	11.5 ft (3.5 m), including tail; stands up to 4 ft (1.2 m) tall
SEXUAL MATURITY	Females 1 year; males about 3 years
LENGTH OF PREGNANCY	331–350 days; weaning at about 6 months
NUMBER OF OFFSPRING	1, very occasionally 2
DIET	Grazes on grass and browses on taller plants
LIFE SPAN	15–20 years

ANIMAL FACTS

The llama is actually a kind of camel. The ancestors of all camels probably originated in North America about 40 million years ago and spread to much of the world. They reached South America about 3 million years ago, where llamas and their close relatives continue to live today. Animals much like llamas lived in North America until about 10,000 years ago. Although these animals died out, people now raise llamas in North America and many other areas. Llamas are close relatives of alpacas, which may have descended from vicuñas.

A llama with its shorter cousin, the alpaca, which is prized for its fine wool.

WHERE IN THE WORLD?

Llamas and their relatives are native to the Andean region of South America, but they are also kept widely throughout the world.

EYELASHES
The llama does not have eyelashes, unlike its close relative, the alpaca.

EARS
Their ears are tall, narrowing along their length. They are often described as banana-shaped.

TAIL
The tail is short and, like the body, is covered in a dense, soft, woolly coat.

BABY LLAMA
A baby llama is called a *cria* (KREE ah).

COLORATION
Llamas are often white, brown, or a mix of these colors.

HOW BIG IS IT?

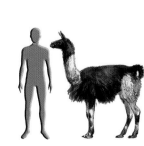

FOUL TEMPER
If frightened or annoyed, llamas spit an unpleasant greenish, grassy fluid.

Kiang

VITAL STATISTICS

WEIGHT	550–880 lb (250–400 kg)
LENGTH	7 ft (2.1 m); with a tail up to 20 in (50 cm) long; up to 4.5 ft (1.3 m) tall
SEXUAL MATURITY	1–2 years
LENGTH OF PREGNANCY	11–12 months
NUMBER OF OFFSPRING	1; weaning occurs at about 12 months
DIET	Grazes on grasses and other low-growing plants on the plains
LIFE SPAN	Up to 20 years

ANIMAL FACTS

The name *kiang* is the word native Tibetans use for this wild ass. Kiangs live in highly structured herds, led by an older female. Males tend to live solitary lives, though younger males form herds over the winter. Mating occurs in the late summer, when food is most plentiful. Pregnant females go off on their own to give birth. The young can run soon afterward, and the mothers and babies rejoin the herd in a few weeks.

This species is the largest of the wild asses. It inhabits some of the most inaccessible terrain on Earth, high on the Tibetan Plateau. It lives in herds of up to 400 individuals.

WHERE IN THE WORLD?

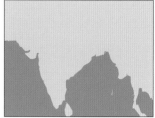

The Tibetan Plateau in Asia, in remote grassland areas at altitudes of 13,123 to 22,966 feet (4,000 to 7,000 meters). Also found in northern Nepal, along the Tibetan border.

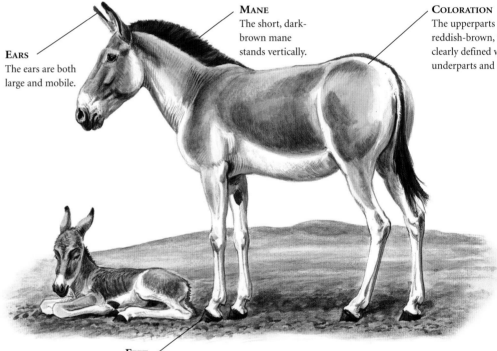

EARS
The ears are both large and mobile.

MANE
The short, dark-brown mane stands vertically.

COLORATION
The upperparts are reddish-brown, with clearly defined white underparts and rump.

FEET
Each foot is actually only a single toe protected by a hoof. The animal runs on the tips of its toes.

Unlike horses, these asses do not spend time grooming each other.

HOW BIG IS IT?

DEFENSE AGAINST ATTACK
Apart from people, wolves are the kiang's only major *predator* (hunting animal). The asses defend themselves by kicking with their hind legs.

Mountain Viscacha

GENUS • *Lagidium*

VITAL STATISTICS

WEIGHT	Can weigh up to 20 lb (9 kg)
LENGTH	20 in (50 cm)
SEXUAL MATURITY	8–12 months for both sexes
LENGTH OF PREGNANCY	120–140 days
NUMBER OF OFFSPRING	1; weaning occurs after about 56 days
DIET	Grass and herbs, including mosses and lichens, but will eat almost any vegetation
LIFE SPAN	6 years; up to 10 in captivity

ANIMAL FACTS

The breeding season of mountain viscachas extends through summer in the Southern Hemisphere, from October to December. Like many other South American rodents, viscachas have a lengthy pregnancy. The youngster is born in an advanced state of development and can feed itself soon after birth, if necessary. Viscachas shelter in *burrows* (underground shelters) and rock crevices. The animal's coloration helps it blend into its rocky habitat.

Chinchillas (above), found in similar terrain, are recognizable by their shorter ears. They are close relatives of viscachas.

These hardy rodents live in groups at high altitudes. They are constantly on the lookout for birds of prey and other *predators* (hunting animals). They are widely hunted by people for their fur and meat.

WHERE IN THE WORLD?

Lives in mountainous country in western South America; can be found in southern Peru, parts of western and central Bolivia, northern and central Chile, and western Argentina.

COLORATION
The body is covered with yellowish-gray fur. The tail has a black tip.

EARS
Tall, flexible ears give viscachas a keen sense of hearing, enabling them to detect predators.

FEET
The front paws can be used like hands to help the viscacha eat.

YOUNG
Young viscachas can feed themselves soon after birth, if necessary.

HOW BIG IS IT?

LOOK-OUT
Members of a group take turns acting as guards to watch for danger as other members feed.

Alpine Marmot

VITAL STATISTICS

WEIGHT	8.8–17.6 lb (4–8 kg); largest of all squirrels
LENGTH	2.1–3 ft (0.6–0.9 m)
SEXUAL MATURITY	1 year
LENGTH OF PREGNANCY	34 days; litters born every 2 years
NUMBER OF OFFSPRING	2–7, typically 3; weaning occurs at 40 days
DIET	Grasses and herbs, seeds and bulbs; also insects, bird eggs, and animal remains
LIFE SPAN	Up to 5 years; 14 in captivity

ANIMAL FACTS

Alpine marmots fatten up in the summer to prepare for the long, bitterly cold winters in their mountain *habitat* (place where an animal lives). As cold weather arrives, marmot families retreat to their *burrows* (underground shelters). The adults plug the entrances to the burrows with soil and dry grass to help keep the interior warm. There, curled up with their offspring, they enter an extended period of *hibernation* (sleeplike state), which can last for up to six months.

These ground squirrels live in grassland areas at high altitudes, sheltering in burrows to escape the worst of the winter weather.

WHERE IN THE WORLD?

Lives in the Swiss, Italian, and French Alps as well as southern Germany and western Austria. Its range extends east to the Carpathian and Tatra mountains. Has been introduced to the Pyrenees.

EARS
These are small and lay flat against the side of the head, reducing the risk of frostbite.

FUR
The dense, brown-gray fur offers excellent protection against the elements.

FRONT PAWS
These are powerful and are equipped with curving claws to aid in digging.

TEETH
The lower *incisor* (cutting) teeth at the front of the mouth are pointed.

HOW BIG IS IT?

BURROWS
Numerous entrances to the tunnels are scattered over the mountainside. The sleeping area is located deep inside.

Plateau Pika

VITAL STATISTICS

WEIGHT	0.2–0.4 lb (0.1–0.2 kg)
LENGTH	5–10 in (12–25 cm)
SEXUAL MATURITY	About 8 months
LENGTH OF PREGNANCY	21–24 days; females produce litters every 3 weeks in the summer
NUMBER OF OFFSPRING	1–8, typically 6; weaning at 21 days
DIET	Eats grass, herbs, flowers, and seeds; may make hay
LIFE SPAN	Can be up to 2.5 years, but most live no more than 3.5 months

ANIMAL FACTS

Highly social by nature, plateau pikas live in groups consisting of a pair with up to 10 offspring from several litters. They inhabit a network of inter-connecting *burrows* (underground shelters), with tunnels extending up to 26 feet (8 meters), with several entrances. The burrows may be shared with other animals, including snowfinches. Plateau pikas are vocal. Members of the group keep in touch with each other as they feed and warn of possible danger.

Staying close to their burrows offers pikas protection from predators.

Pikas are relatives of rabbits, found at high altitudes throughout northern areas of the world. Their name comes from an Asiatic word that describes their squeaking call.

WHERE IN THE WORLD?

Plateau pikas are found at high altitudes, inhabiting the meadows and steppe areas of the Tibetan Plateau, in the Chang Taung region of China.

COLORATION
The top of the body and head are brown to tan in color. The belly and legs are grayish-white.

NOSE
The dark coloration here extends around the lips.

APPEARANCE
Pikas are short-legged and stocky and do not have a tail. The sexes look much the same.

PAWS
These are quite broad and end in small, dark claws.

HOW BIG IS IT?

MAKING HAY
Plateau pikas collect vegetation that they leave to dry so that it becomes hay. The hay keeps them alive during the bitterly cold winter.

Mountain Lion

VITAL STATISTICS

WEIGHT	Females 75–105 lb (34–48 kg); males 115–160 lb (53–72 kg)
LENGTH	5–9 ft (1.5–2.7 m), including tail; up to 30 in (76 cm) tall
SEXUAL MATURITY	18–36 months
LENGTH OF PREGNANCY	91 days
NUMBER OF OFFSPRING	Average 2–3, but can be up to 5–6; weaning occurs at 90 days
DIET	Hunts mainly medium-sized mammals
LIFE SPAN	Probably 8–10 years; up to 20 years in captivity

ANIMAL FACTS

Mountain lions have an amazing ability to jump, thanks to their powerful hind legs. They can leap horizontally up to 40 feet (12 meters), and they may spring up to 18 feet (5.5 meters) into the air. Their athletic skills also include sprinting over short distances at speeds up to 34 miles (55 kilometers) per hour. Mountain lions have the biggest range of any land animal in the Americas. People have moved into many mountain lion *habitats* (living areas), which has contributed to rare mountain lion attacks on people.

Young mountain lions have spotted coats.

The mountain lion is known by more than 40 different names, including cougar, panther, and puma. Except for the jaguar, the mountain lion is the largest cat in the Western Hemisphere.

WHERE IN THE WORLD?

Ranges from western Canada down through the western United States (with a small population in Florida), across Central America and through almost all of South America.

EYES
These are pointed forward, helping the mountain lion pinpoint the position of its prey with great accuracy.

FACE
The face is rounded and the neck is very muscular.

COMMUNICATIONS
Unlike most other large cats, mountain lions cannot roar. But they can purr as smaller cats do. The cry of the mountain lion sounds like a person screaming. The cats also can make hissing and whistlelike noises.

PAWS
Five retractable claws on each front foot help the mountain lion maintain its balance when jumping or climbing.

HOW BIG IS IT?

CAUGHT UNAWARE
Mountain lions try to ambush prey—often deer—rather than pursue it. They move very quietly, making use of any available cover.

Snow Leopard

VITAL STATISTICS

WEIGHT	75–120 lb (34–54 kg)
LENGTH	5.9–7.6 ft (1.8–2.3 m), including tail; up to 2 ft (0.6 m) tall
SEXUAL MATURITY	24 months
LENGTH OF PREGNANCY	95–100 days
NUMBER OF OFFSPRING	Average 2–3, but can be 5; weaning occurs at around 180 days
DIET	Hunts wild sheep, deer, and boar, plus rodents and livestock
LIFE SPAN	15 years; up to 20 in captivity

ANIMAL FACTS

These wild cats roam above the snow line during the summer. The snow line is the lower edge of the permanent snowfields found on upper mountain slopes. In the winter, snow leopards move to lower altitudes and live in forests. They are well-protected against the cold, with fur covering their paws. They sleep curled up in a ball, with their long tail protecting their exposed nose and mouth from the bitter cold.

Snow leopard patterning

Leopard patterning

Solitary by nature, the snow leopard is an elusive species, living in remote mountains. Unfortunately, it has become endangered, with fewer than 7,000 of the cats surviving in the wild.

WHERE IN THE WORLD?

Ranges across the mountainous regions of central Asia, from 6,500 to 20,000 feet (2,000 to 6,000 meters), through the Himalaya and Tibet into western China.

EYES
Keen eyesight helps snow leopards detect the movement of potential prey.

COMMUNICATING
Snow leopards cannot roar, but they yowl loudly. They also make scrapes in the soil with their back legs and spray boulders with a strong scent. These signals warn away other snow leopards. The signals also help males and females find each other in the mating season.

COATS
Dark brown spots and black rosettes cover a whitish-tan base. Snow leopards are hunted for their beautiful pelts, as well as their bones and organs, though buying and selling such parts is illegal.

TAIL
Long and strong, the tail acts as a counterbalance when jumping.

GETTING AROUND
Snow leopards are incredibly agile animals despite their size. They can leap easily across rocky outcrops.

HOW BIG IS IT?

Spectacled Bear

VITAL STATISTICS

WEIGHT	141–341 lb (64–155 kg); males are heavier
LENGTH	4–5 ft (1.2–1.5 m); about 28 in (71 cm) tall
SEXUAL MATURITY	4–7 years
LENGTH OF PREGNANCY	200–260 days
NUMBER OF OFFSPRING	2–3; weaning takes place around 18 months
DIET	Feeds on fruit, berries, plants, nuts, seeds, small animals, and animal remains
LIFE SPAN	Up to 25 years; as long as 36 years recorded in captivity

The spectacled bear is the only bear species native to South America. These bears have striking patterns around their eyes, which may make them look as though they are wearing spectacles, or eyeglasses.

WHERE IN THE WORLD?

Ranges from Panama in Central America through Colombia, Venezuela, Peru, and Ecuador to parts of Bolivia, Brazil, and Argentina, favoring mountainous areas.

ANIMAL FACTS

Spectacled bears live in a range of *habitats* (living areas), but they favor *cloud forests* in the mountains. Cloud forests are dense forests in tropical areas that are almost constantly covered by clouds. The bears spend much of their time in trees. Spectacled bears are smaller than many other bear species. They are also different in having only 13 pairs of ribs, rather than 14. Other species of bears once lived in South America, but only the spectacled bear remains. Overhunting and the destruction of its forest home have made this bear scarce throughout much of its range.

HEAD
The jaws are short, and the facial markings are a combination of white and yellow fur.

DIET
The bear eats mainly fruit, leaves, and roots.

PAWS
The paws are powerful and equipped with sharp claws, enabling these bears to dig effectively.

COLORATION
Fur is black or dark brown and dense, giving good protection against the elements.

FACIAL PATTERNS
These bears can differ markedly in appearance, with only some showing the areas of pale fur around the eyes that give the bears their name.

HOW BIG IS IT?

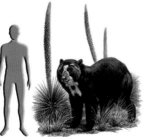

Spectacled bears are good swimmers as well as good climbers.

North American Black Bear

These bears favor thickly forested mountainous areas. They are highly territorial, with individual males occupying areas of up to 40 square miles (100 square kilometers).

VITAL STATISTICS

WEIGHT	200–600 lb (90–270 kg); males are heavier
LENGTH	5.5–6 ft (1.6–1.9 m); about 3 ft (0.9 m) tall
SEXUAL MATURITY	3–4 years, but may not breed until age 7
LENGTH OF PREGNANCY	Around 220 days
NUMBER OF OFFSPRING	2–3; weaning takes place around 6–8 months
DIET	Feeds on fruits, berries, plants, nuts, seeds, carrion, fish, and deer
LIFE SPAN	Up to 32 years

ANIMAL FACTS

The black bear is the smallest of the three *species* (kinds) of North American bear. The cubs are tiny at birth, weighing as little as 8 ounces (220 grams). But they grow rapidly on their mother's rich milk. By the time they emerge from their den in the spring, they may have grown to 11 pounds (5 kilograms). Young bears face a variety of threats, including adult male bears, which may seek to kill cubs so they can produce their own cubs with the mother.

North American black bears are skillful at climbing trees to escape danger.

WHERE IN THE WORLD?

Found across northern North America, extending through the western United States to northern Mexico. Also in parts of the Midwest and East.

MUZZLE
This is broad, and covered in short, light-colored hair.

HINDQUARTERS
The hindquarters are muscular, with a hard-to-see tail.

COLORATION
Color varies from cinnamon to darker brown to black. Occasional white individuals have been recorded.

FEET
Like other bears, black bears walk on the soles of their feet, with the heels touching the ground. Black bears can run as fast as 25 miles (40 kilometers) per hour when chasing prey.

HOW BIG IS IT?

SCAVENGING
Black bears may become troublesome around camps and cabins if food is left in their reach. They have severely injured and, rarely, killed campers or travelers who feed them.

Golden Eagle

These magnificent eagles are spectacular flyers, able to attain speeds of 80 miles (128 kilometers) per hour when pursuing prey. They most commonly live in mountainous areas.

VITAL STATISTICS

WEIGHT	6.5–13.5 lb (3–6.1 kg); hens are larger
LENGTH	2.5–3 ft (0.7–0.9 cm); wingspan 6–7.2 ft (1.8–2.2 m)
SEXUAL MATURITY	5 years
NUMBER OF EGGS	2, white with darker markings
INCUBATION PERIOD	About 45 days; young fledge after about 50 days
DIET	Hunts birds and such mammals as rabbits; sometimes eats animal remains
LIFE SPAN	Up to 38 years in the wild; 50 in captivity

ANIMAL FACTS

Golden eagles bond with their mates for several years. These pairs occupy large *territories* (home areas), which can extend up to 35 square miles (56 square kilometers). When breeding, they construct a large, bulky nest, often on a rocky crag or in a tree. The pair return to the same site every year, adding to the nest. People once killed many golden eagles because ranchers mistakenly feared the birds would kill many young lambs. Golden eagles are now protected by law in many of the areas where they live.

A feared hunter

WHERE IN THE WORLD?

Sometimes found in Western Europe and North Africa, and from Scandinavia across Asia. Also found in North America, from Alaska to Mexico, but less common in eastern areas.

EYES
Golden eagles have sharp vision that enables them to spot prey from a distance.

BILL
The large, powerful bill has a hooked tip to hold on to prey and rip flesh from a carcass.

COLORATION
Color varies in individuals, ranging from a consistent dark to golden brown.

TAIL
The tail feathers are broad and short, with slightly rounded tips.

LIFTING ABILITY
The feet of the golden eagle are equipped with powerful claws called talons. The bird uses its talons to carry prey back to its nest.

HOW BIG IS IT?

FLYING UNDER THE RADAR

After spotting potential prey, a golden eagle will fly low over the landscape, using the terrain as cover.

Andean Condor

VITAL STATISTICS

WEIGHT	17.5–33 lb (39–73 kg); males are much heavier than females
LENGTH	3.5–4.3 ft (1–1.3 m); wingspan 10.1 ft (3.1 m)
SEXUAL MATURITY	6 years
NUMBER OF EGGS	1, white, measuring about 4 in (10 cm) long
INCUBATION PERIOD	About 59 days; young fledge after about 180 days
DIET	Feeds mainly on the remains of mammals, including marine mammals washed ashore
LIFE SPAN	50 years

This vulture is one of the world's largest flying birds. Its huge wingspan helps it to glide almost effortlessly on rising currents of hot air called thermals.

WHERE IN THE WORLD?

Lives in western South America, along the Andes Mountains but will forage further afield over open country and coasts. It is not seen in forested areas.

ANIMAL FACTS

Mountains are important to these gigantic vultures, which use them as launch pads. The warmth of the morning sun creates rising currents of hot air. Riding these thermals allows condors to maintain their altitude with very little effort. As a result, they can glide for long periods, flapping their wings only about once every hour. Nesting on rugged peaks also protects the chicks from *predators* (hunting animals).

Andean condors often feed in groups.

WINGS
These have an immense span when fully extended, with long flight feathers.

HEAD
An absence of plumage on the head allows this bird to feed without getting its feathers matted by blood.

BILL
The condor uses its powerful and sharply curved bill to tear strips of meat from animal remains.

FEET
The condor's toes cannot grasp food, so feeding must take place on the ground.

MARINE PREY
Condors often search beaches for dead seals and similar creatures. Occasionally, they may kill prey.

HOW BIG IS IT?

SEEKING FOOD
While soaring over the open landscape, the condor uses its keen eyesight to search for carcasses on the ground. The sight of other condors in an area is an indication of the presence of food.

Alpine Salamander

VITAL STATISTICS

LENGTH	3.5–6 in (9–15 cm); females are slightly larger than males
SEXUAL MATURITY	4–5 years
HATCHING PERIOD	The young develop inside the female, with eggs carried for 2–3 years before birth
NUMBER OF OFFSPRING	2
HABITAT	Damp alpine meadows and woodland
DIET	Hunts worms and other small animals, feeding in the water and on land
LIFE SPAN	10–15 years

ANIMAL FACTS

Most *species* (types) of salamander lay their eggs in water, but the unusual breeding habits of Alpine salamanders enable them to survive in areas without bodies of water. Alpine salamanders also can survive the cold mountain climate, because they *hibernate* (enter a sleeplike state) through the long winter. They normally hunt at night and are especially active after rainfall.

Not all members of this species are black. The golden Alpine salamander from northern Italy has bright yellow markings on its back.

Venom protects these salamanders from predators.

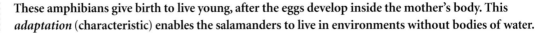

These amphibians give birth to live young, after the eggs develop inside the mother's body. This *adaptation* (characteristic) enables the salamanders to live in environments without bodies of water.

WHERE IN THE WORLD?

Lives in mountainous areas throughout much of Central Europe, extending as far east as Bosnia-Herzegovina and Serbia, at altitudes of up to 9,186 feet (2,800 meters).

COLORATION
The glossy black appearance explains why this species is also called the black salamander.

PAROTID GLANDS
These swollen areas behind the eyes are the openings of glands that secrete *venom* (poison) for defense against enemies.

WINTER SURVIVAL
A cold *habitat* (area) keeps these salamanders in hibernation for up to eight months of the year.

PROTECTIVE POISON
Parallel rows of protective venom glands run down the back on each side of the body.

HIND LEGS
These are often kept flattened and extended, away from the body.

BREEDING STRATEGY
Alpine salamanders produce far fewer offspring than most other amphibians. The young look like miniature adults.

HOW BIG IS IT?

Alpine Newt

VITAL STATISTICS

LENGTH	3–5 in (8–12 cm)
SEXUAL MATURITY	2–3 years
NUMBER OF EGGS	75–200; development of young depends on temperature, sometimes overwintering as tadpoles in mountainous areas
HABITAT	Damp areas, especially woodland
DIET	Hunts small *invertebrates* (animals without backbones) in water and on land
LIFE SPAN	6–8 years

ANIMAL FACTS

There are several *subspecies* (varieties) of Alpine newt, which vary in size, body shape, and coloration. The subspecies developed because different groups of the animal became trapped in isolated areas at the end of the last ice age. Since then, they have started to develop different *adaptations* (characteristics), depending on their environments. Many varieties of Alpine newt live in only one small area and are endangered.

The female deposits each egg under the leaves of an aquatic plant.

Alpine newts have a complex life cycle. Tadpoles hatch from eggs that the females lay underwater. These mature into salamanders that live on land. But the newts return to the water during the breeding season.

WHERE IN THE WORLD?

Lives in Alpine regions and in lowland areas from Belgium to eastern Russia and south to Greece.

BREEDING COLORATION
During the breeding season, males develop a crest along their back and brilliant blue coloring on the flanks and tail.

TAIL
The tail is broad and flat, tapering along its length to a point.

LEGS
The legs of a newt are weak.

EYES
The eyes are brightly colored and relatively large; newts rely partly on their eyesight to locate prey.

FEMALE
Females are duller in appearance, with speckling extending down to the underparts, which are paler yellow.

OUT OF THE WATER
Alpine newts leave the water after the breeding season and appear less colorful throughout the rest of the year.

HOW BIG IS IT?

DEVELOPMENT OF TADPOLES

Tadpoles use gills to breathe underwater. As they mature, they lose their gills and begin to use lungs to breathe air on land. They are then known as efts.

Musk Ox

VITAL STATISTICS

WEIGHT	400–835 lb (180–380 kg)
LENGTH	7–8.5 ft (2.1–2.6 m), including tail
SEXUAL MATURITY	Females 3–4 years; males 5–6 years
LENGTH OF PREGNANCY	About 255 days
NUMBER OF OFFSPRING	Generally 1, occasionally twins; weaning occurs at 10–18 months
DIET	Grazes on grass and sedges; browses on shrubs
LIFE SPAN	Typically 20–24 years

ANIMAL FACTS

Musk oxen undertake what is known as a reverse migration. They do not travel to more sheltered lowland areas at the approach of the bitter Arctic winter. Instead, they migrate to the bleak, exposed uplands, where the winds help expose grasses and other low-growing plants. The oxen's presence often attracts wolves, which try to overpower young calves. When threatened, the adults form a circle, corralling the calves in the center. This often deters any attack, as adults can kill wolves with their horns.

Female (left) and male (right)

In the 1800's and early 1900's, people hunted musk oxen almost to extinction. In 1917, Canada enacted laws to protect these animals. Today, large herds roam again in Arctic Canada as well as Greenland.

WHERE IN THE WORLD?

Lives in parts of western and northern Alaska, through northern Canada west of Hudson Bay and up to Greenland, where it is more common in western areas.

LEGS
The legs are free of longer hair, helping the musk ox to move through snow more easily.

HOOFS
Broad *cloven* (divided) hoofs help musk oxen scrape through snow to reach grass and other plants during the long Arctic winter.

HORNS
The horns are low-set on the central area over the top of the head, called the boss.

COAT
Individual hairs may measure up to 24 inches (61 centimeters) long and trail almost to the ground.

STAYING SAFE

As wolves attack, the oxen form a circle, with any calves in the middle. One of the adults charges the wolves with its head down, while the others maintain the defensive shield around the young.

HOW BIG IS IT?

Caribou

VITAL STATISTICS

WEIGHT	240-700 lb 109-118 kg)
LENGTH	6.4–7.75 ft (1.9–2.3 m), including tail; up to 4 ft (1.2 m) tall
SEXUAL MATURITY	2–3 years
LENGTH OF PREGNANCY	About 227 days; weaning occurs 4–5 months later
NUMBER OF OFFSPRING	1
DIET	Browses on lichens, shrubs, and similar food
LIFE SPAN	Typically about 5 years, but can be up to 15

ANIMAL FACTS

Herds of caribou undertake seasonal migrations in the far north in search of food. They head to the Arctic plains when the snow there thaws in the summer. Up to 200,000 individuals have been recorded in a single herd, though herds usually number less than 10,000. The young are born in the summer, and they can run almost at once. This helps them to escape such *predators* (hunting animals) as polar bears and wolves. Young caribou lack the white spots common on other young deer.

Caribou hoofs have four "toes." The larger toes are spread out to help the caribou walk on snow.

These deer are unusual in that both sexes have antlers. Caribou actually belong to the same *species* (type) as reindeer, which live in Europe and Asia. But reindeer are often heavier and have shorter legs.

WHERE IN THE WORLD?

Herds of wild caribou live throughout much of Alaska and Canada, with some in northern Idaho and Washington. They typically migrate with the changing seasons.

COLORATION
The caribou's appearance changes with the seasons. They are brownish in summer, and become grayer in winter.

THROAT POUCHES
The male has two inflatable sacs that increase the sound of his roaring during the breeding period.

CHANGING WITH THE SEASONS
In winter, the outside edge of the hoof grows harder to help the caribou walk on ice and snow. In summer, the sole of the foot becomes softer for walking on rocky land.

NOSE
The caribou's sense of smell is vital to its survival, helping it locate food buried beneath the snow.

COAT
The coat is thick and is very effective in trapping air close to the skin, helping to insulate the caribou from the cold.

HOW BIG IS IT?

Caribou   Reindeer

DOMESTIC COUSINS
People in northern Europe keep reindeer as livestock. They use reindeer skin for boots, clothing, and tents. They also drink reindeer milk and eat reindeer meat.

Norwegian Lemming

VITAL STATISTICS

WEIGHT	0.5–4.5 oz (20–130 g)
LENGTH	4–6 in (10–15 cm)
SEXUAL MATURITY	From around 14 days
LENGTH OF PREGNANCY	Typically 16 days; 3–6 litters annually
NUMBER OF OFFSPRING	4–12; weaning occurs at around 12 days
DIET	Grass, herbs, moss, lichens, leaves, berries, and bark
LIFE SPAN	Typically up to 2 years

ANIMAL FACTS

Lemmings are rapid breeders. Their numbers can build up quickly in an area, even though their food supply is limited and often scarce. As a result, lemmings suffer mass die-offs, caused by severe winter weather, diseases, and behavioral changes due to stress. After a population crash, their numbers then build up again, and the cycle repeats itself. The cycle usually lasts about four years. The mass die-offs of lemmings inspired false stories that the animals threw themselves from cliffs.

A common belief about lemmings is that a large group of the animals may follow their leader off a cliff to their death. However, lemmings do not deliberately kill themselves.

WHERE IN THE WORLD?

Lives throughout Scandinavia, extending into adjacent areas of Russia. Often seen near water.

HARE LIP
The upper lip is split. Sharp *incisor* (cutting) teeth are located at the front of the mouth.

FUR
This is waterproof and offers good insulation against the cold.

COLORATION
The color provides camouflage, helping the lemmings blend in with the landscape.

LEGS
These enable lemmings to *burrow* (dig) under the snow in search of food, creating underground tunnels.

A VITAL FOOD SOURCE
Lemmings provide food for such *predators* (hunting animals) as snowy owls, whose population is directly linked to that of lemmings in some areas.

HOW BIG IS IT?

Ermine

Ermine are fierce *predators* (hunting animals) that have long been prized for the beautiful white fur they grow in the winter. Ermine are also known as stoats.

VITAL STATISTICS

WEIGHT	2–10 oz (0.06-0.28 kg)
LENGTH	7–13 in (18–33 cm); up to 12 in (30 cm) tall
SEXUAL MATURITY	Females 2 months; males 2 years
LENGTH OF PREGNANCY	42–56 days; development is delayed after fertilization
NUMBER OF OFFSPRING	Averages 2, ranges from 1–4; weaning occurs at 9 weeks
DIET	Hunts small mammals, especially rabbits, plus other small creatures
LIFE SPAN	3–11 years; up to 26 years in captivity

WHERE IN THE WORLD?

Found in areas, up to the edge of the Arctic Circle, across North America and through Europe to Asia. Has been introduced to Australia and New Zealand.

ANIMAL FACTS

Ermine turn white in the winter, helping them to merge into a snowy landscape. Shy by nature, these animals rarely stray far from cover. They have a number of *burrows* (underground shelters) throughout their *territory* (home area). They are fierce and aggressive, so they are rarely attacked by other predators. Foxes, badgers, and birds of prey sometimes eat ermines. Female ermines may mate when they are just a few weeks old, but they do not give birth until the following year.

Ermine may hunt relatively large prey, including rabbits.

WHISKERS
These help ermine to feel their way through burrows, where they hunt rodents.

COLORATION
Upperparts are ginger to brownish; the belly and throat vary from white to cream.

FRONT FEET
Large and powerful, the feet have sharp claws at the end of the toes.

TAIL
Relatively short, the tail always has a black tip, even in winter.

COLORATION THROUGH THE SEASONS

In some cases, ermine only partially change color in the autumn. Females are a purer shade of white than males.

HOW BIG IS IT?

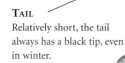

Wolverine

The wolverine is the largest member of the weasel family. It is both a powerful *predator* (hunting animal) and a scavenger. Its scientific name means *glutton*, a reference to its large appetite.

VITAL STATISTICS

WEIGHT	24–55 lb (11–25 kg); males are heavier
LENGTH	26–34 in (66–86 cm); up to 17 in (43 cm) tall
SEXUAL MATURITY	1–2 years
LENGTH OF PREGNANCY	About 50 days; development does not begin right after fertilization
NUMBER OF OFFSPRING	2–3; weaning occurs at around 70 days
DIET	Will steal from such predators as wolves and hunts prey up to the size of a moose
LIFE SPAN	10–13 years in the wild; up to 18 in captivity

ANIMAL FACTS

The wolverine is also called the skunk bear because of its unpleasant odor. Individuals roam over very large *territories* (home areas). A male's territory can extend 240 square miles (620 square kilometers). Females have a territory of 100 square miles (260 square kilometers). Mating occurs in summer, but the pregnancy does not start to develop until winter, ensuring that young are born in the spring.

Wolverines are able to climb well.

WHERE IN THE WORLD?

Lives throughout northern areas, from North America to Europe and Asia.

EARS
The small ears are well-insulated by fur.

FUR
Brown with yellow streaking on the flanks, the thick fur offers good protection against the cold.

TEETH
A rotated *molar* (grinding) tooth at the back of each jaw is used to crush bones and strip frozen meat from animal remains.

FEET
The feet are equipped with formidable claws, used for fighting and ripping apart prey.

HOW BIG IS IT?

POWERFUL KILLER

Wolverines are powerful despite their relatively small size. In the winter, they hunt animals as large as moose. A wolverine kills large prey by jumping on the animal's back and holding on until the animal falls.

Siberian Tiger

This is the largest of the nine kinds of tiger, and it is the biggest member of the cat family. Unfortunately, only a small number of the cats survive because of illegal hunting and a loss of habitat.

VITAL STATISTICS

WEIGHT	Females 220–397 lb (100–180 kg); males 368–932 lb (167–432 kg)
LENGTH	9.5–10.5 ft (2.9–3.2 m), including tail; up to 4 ft (1.2 m) tall
SEXUAL MATURITY	3 years
LENGTH OF PREGNANCY	90–105 days
NUMBER OF OFFSPRING	Average 3–4, but can be up to 6; weaning occurs at 90 days
DIET	Hunts a variety of animals; prefers larger mammals
LIFE SPAN	Probably 10–12 years, although can live up to 23

WHERE IN THE WORLD?

Used to range throughout northeastern China, parts of Mongolia and Russia, and the Korean Peninsula. Now confined mainly to the Amur-Ussuri region of Russia.

ANIMAL FACTS

The number of these tigers plummeted over the past century, largely because of hunting. They died out in South Korea in 1922 and are rare in China. Thanks to determined conservation efforts, several hundred survive in Russia. The strength of these tigers is such that adults can overpower even bears easily, though they more frequently hunt red deer and wild boar.

COLORATION
Siberian tigers have whiter fur alongside areas of gold, rather than bright orange fur.

STRIPES
Stripes are less apparent in Siberian tigers and are generally brown rather than black.

MANE
These tigers develop a substantial mane of longer fur around the neck in winter.

FUR
The fur is very dense, with around 3,000 hairs per square centimeter over the body.

GIVING BIRTH
Female tigers usually give birth to two or three cubs. Newborn cubs are dependent on their mother for food until they are about a year old. Cubs become fully independent at about 2 years old.

Tigers lap up water with their tongue, like a domestic cat.

HOW BIG IS IT?

Arctic Fox

VITAL STATISTICS

WEIGHT	2–20 lb (1–9 kg); males are heavier than females
LENGTH	About 20 in (50 cm)
SEXUAL MATURITY	2 years
LENGTH OF PREGNANCY	52 days
NUMBER OF OFFSPRING	6–15; weaning occurs at 35–63 days
DIET	Eats birds, eggs, fish, lemmings, and berries; scavenges on the remains of such large marine mammals as seals
LIFE SPAN	5–7 years in the wild; up to 10 in captivity

ANIMAL FACTS

Arctic foxes live where there are no trees to provide cover, so they rely on their coloration to conceal their presence. Most Arctic foxes change color from brown or gray in summer to white in winter. They live in *burrows* (underground shelers), sometimes in small groups, though there is likely to be a dominant pair that mates for life. Other group members help to raise the offspring. Arctic foxes are well-insulated against the cold. Even the soles of their feet are covered with fur, to protect them from frostbite.

In summer, the fox's coat may become darker in color.

Found farther north than any other member of the dog family, the Arctic fox is well-adapted to this incredibly harsh environment.

WHERE IN THE WORLD?

Lives in the far north, extending across the Arctic. Can be found in Alaska, northern Canada, and Greenland, as well as in northern Europe and Asia.

MUZZLE
The short muzzle prevents heat loss. The nose is black, as are the claws.

COLORATION
Not all Arctic foxes are white; some are grayish-brown.

TAIL
The fur covering the tail is dense, giving it a bushy appearance.

HUNTING
Arctic foxes are highly flexible in their feeding habits, scavenging on animal remains and sometimes attacking seal pups.

HOW BIG IS IT?

Kodiak Bear

SPECIES • *Ursus arctos middendorffi*

Kodiaks are the largest of the brown bears, found throughout the islands of southwestern Alaska. Kodiak bears usually avoid people, but they can be dangerous if disturbed or stressed.

VITAL STATISTICS

WEIGHT	350–1,500 lb (159–680 kg); males are heavier than females
LENGTH	6–9.5 ft (1.8–2.9 m); about 5 ft (1.5 m) tall
SEXUAL MATURITY	5–7 years; males may not breed until 10
LENGTH OF PREGNANCY	186–248 days; development begins 5 months after fertilization
NUMBER OF OFFSPRING	1–5, normally 2; weaning occurs at 6–8 months
DIET	Eats fruit, vegetation, animal remains, and salmon
LIFE SPAN	20–30 years; 40 in captivity

ANIMAL FACTS

The lives of Kodiak bears are closely linked to their environment. In the fall, they start to enter dens, where they spend the winter *hibernating* (remaining in a sleeplike state), relying on their body fat to sustain them. By the following spring, the bears may have lost one-third of their body weight. In the spring and summer, they fatten up again. Kodiak bears have a varied diet, but summer salmon runs are an especially important food source. The bears mate in midsummer, but the development of the young is delayed. The cubs are born early the following year. At birth, a cub is about the size of a rat.

WHERE IN THE WORLD?

Lives in southwestern Alaska, on offshore islands including Kodiak, Shuyak, and Afognak, and on the Alaskan mainland.

COLORATION
Individuals from southerly areas, including females, are lighter in color.

HEIGHT
These bears stand up to 13 feet (4 meters) tall on their hind legs.

CLAWS
The claws are black but often turn whitish in older bears. They are about 5 inches (13 centimeters) long.

HIND PAWS
These are massive, measuring up to 16 inches (41 centimeters) long. They support the bear's great weight when it stands.

STANDING OUT
Kodiak bears have a distinctive profile. Genetic studies suggest they have not mated with other types of brown bears for more than 10,000 years.

Brown bear

Kodiak bear

HOW BIG IS IT?

DENNING
These bears may dig their own dens or enlarge existing holes.

Polar Bear

VITAL STATISTICS

WEIGHT	900–1,600 lb (410–720 kg); males are heavier than females
LENGTH	6–10 ft (1.90–3 m); about 5.25 ft (1.6 m) tall
SEXUAL MATURITY	4–6 years; males mate after 8 years
LENGTH OF PREGNANCY	195–265 days; development begins 4 months after fertilization
NUMBER OF OFFSPRING	1–4; weaning occurs at 18–30 months
DIET	Hunts mainly seals, plus fish, reindeer, animal remains, and vegetation in summer
LIFE SPAN	20–30 years; 45 in captivity

Polar bears are the largest of all bears, and they also are the largest *predators* (hunting animals) on land. The bears are excellent swimmers. They mainly hunt seals from the Arctic sea ice.

WHERE IN THE WORLD?

Polar bears live in regions where the sea freezes in winter, chiefly along the northern coasts and islands of Alaska, Canada, Greenland, Norway, and Russia.

FUR
The bear's distinctive creamy-white fur blends into the landscape and is water-repellant.

NOSE
The nose is highly sensitive, allowing the bear to detect a seal carcass up to 20 miles (32 kilometers) away.

HIND LEGS
The hind legs, which are longer than the front legs, are used for swimming.

FEET
Covered with hair, the feet act as snowshoes, helping the bear to walk on snow and ice without suffering frostbite.

ANIMAL FACTS

A thick layer of *blubber* (fat) protects polar bears from the cold. Females give birth in dens dug in the snow, where the temperature is warmer than outside. The continued loss of sea ice due to global warming could pose a major threat to these bears. They live on and hunt mainly from the sea ice. In the summer, the bears must swim longer distances to reach the remaining ice.

The underside of a polar bear's foot is protected by hair (left), compared with that of a brown bear (right).

HOW BIG IS IT?

HUNTING TECHNIQUE

Polar bears can locate an air hole in the ice made by a seal from more than 1 mile (1.6 kilometers) away. They then wait patiently for the seal to surface.

Sea Otter

SPECIES • *Enhydra lutris*

VITAL STATISTICS

WEIGHT	60–85 lb (27–39 kg); males are heavier than females
LENGTH	4–5 ft (1.2–1.5 m)
SEXUAL MATURITY	2–5 years
LENGTH OF PREGNANCY	Up to 270 days, as development may not begin right after fertilization
NUMBER OF OFFSPRING	1, occasionally 2; weaning takes 6–12 months
DIET	Mollusks, clams, sea urchins obtained from the sea bed, and fish
LIFE SPAN	10–20 years in the wild; up to 28 in captivity

ANIMAL FACTS

Sea otters are well-suited to ocean life. Their thick fur has an undercoat that traps air close to the body. This helps them to float and keep warm. Sea otters can swim very well. They may use stones to smash open shellfish. Sea otters are vital to the health of kelp forests because they eat sea urchins that damage the kelp. Females carry their young on their chest when resting and leave them floating on the surface while they dive.

Diving in search of shellfish and other food

Sea otters live among kelp forests—dense areas of giant seaweed—and rarely come ashore. They float on their backs when not swimming.

WHERE IN THE WORLD?

Inshore areas on both sides of the Bering Sea and around the Aleutian Islands between Russia and Alaska, extending down as far as California in the United States.

LEGS
The legs are very short. The front legs are used like hands for holding food.

WHISKERS
These sensory hairs are prominent around the mouth and above the eyes.

HIND FEET
The sea otter swims using its flipper-shaped hind feet as paddles.

COLORATION
Sea otters are dark brown overall, with paler fur on the head.

EARS
The ears are very small and set low down on the sides of the head.

HOW BIG IS IT?

SLEEPING SECURELY

Sea otters anchor themselves among beds of kelp so they will not drift in the current when sleeping.

Bearded Seal

VITAL STATISTICS

WEIGHT	440–800 lb (200–360 kg); females are slightly heavier than males
LENGTH	7–8 ft (2.1–2.4 m)
SEXUAL MATURITY	Females 3–8 years; males 6–7 years
LENGTH OF PREGNANCY	248–279 days; development only starts 2–3 months after fertilization
NUMBER OF OFFSPRING	1; weaning occurs by 18 days
DIET	Eats mainly clams, crabs, and other animals on the sea floor; also hunts fish including sculpin and cod
LIFE SPAN	25–30 years

ANIMAL FACTS

These seals are solitary by nature. They live among broken areas of ice, moving farther north in summer as the ice melts. Bearded seals favor relatively shallow waters, down to depths of about 427 feet (130 meters), seeking their food at or near the bottom. They use their whiskers to detect shellfish and mollusks. Their major *predator* (hunting animal) is the polar bear, which ambushes the seals at breathing holes in the ice.

Front flipper, showing the digits and claws in detail

The name of this seal comes from the prominent rows of long, pale, spiralling whiskers on its snout. These whiskers look something like a beard.

WHERE IN THE WORLD?

Lives in the North Atlantic, the western Laptev and Barents seas, and in the rest of the Arctic Sea. Also found in the Bering and Okhotsk seas.

BODY SHAPE
Although the seal is somewhat cumbersome on land, its streamlined shape helps it to swim well.

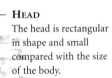

HEAD
The head is rectangular in shape and small compared with the size of the body.

COAT
A dense layer of underfur and protective *blubber* (fat) provide insulation against the ice and cold.

COLORATION
Dark, typically varying from gray to brown, with no patterning.

FROSTY BREATHING
As mammals, bearded seals must breathe air. They use their claws to create breathing holes in the ice.

OUT OF THE WATER
Bearded seals rest on drifting *ice floes* (chunks of ice). Females also give birth on the floes.

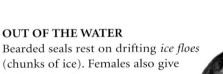

HOW BIG IS IT?

Leopard Seal

SPECIES • *Hydrurga leptonyx*

VITAL STATISTICS

WEIGHT	630–1,100 lb (295–500 kg); females are heavier than males
LENGTH	10–12 ft (3–3.7 m)
SEXUAL MATURITY	Females 3–8 years; males 6–7 years
LENGTH OF PREGNANCY	248–279 days; development only starts 2–3 months after fertilization
NUMBER OF OFFSPRING	1; weaning occurs by 18 days
DIET	Hunts penguins, other seals; also feeds on squid and krill
LIFE SPAN	12–15 years

ANIMAL FACTS

Solitary by nature, leopard seals wander on and around the Antarctic pack ice, heading farther north in winter. They are fearsome hunters, feeding on penguins and seals. They kill penguins by battering them ferociously from side to side in the water. The leopard seal's *molars* (grinding teeth) also act as sieves, enabling them to feed on tiny, shrimplike krill. Leopard seals themselves face few predators, apart from occasional attacks by killer whales.

A leopard seal on an ice floe.

These seals get their name from their spotted coat, which somewhat resembles that of a leopard. Like their namesake, leopard seals are fearsome *predators* (hunting animals).

WHERE IN THE WORLD?

Found on the pack ice in Antarctic waters, and occasionally recorded as venturing farther north to Australia, New Zealand, South Africa, and South America.

EARS
Although leopard seals lack visible earflaps, they have ears and excellent hearing.

MOUTH
Its large mouth can open wide and is filled with an array of sharp teeth.

BODY
The body is narrow, with a distinctive spotted pattern, particularly prominent on the underparts.

FLIPPERS
These are relatively long, aiding both the swimming power and agility of these seals.

HOW BIG IS IT?

HUNTING TECHNIQUE
The leopard seal lurks beneath an ice shelf, waiting for a penguin to dive into the water. Then the seal strikes.

Southern Elephant Seal

VITAL STATISTICS

WEIGHT	1,100–8,800 lb (500–4,000 kg); males are larger than females
LENGTH	6.6–22.5 ft (2–6.9 m)
SEXUAL MATURITY	Females 2–4 years; males 3–6 years but unlikely to breed before age 10
LENGTH OF PREGNANCY	About 266 days; development starts 3 months after fertilization
NUMBER OF OFFSPRING	1; weaning occurs by 23 days
DIET	Mainly squid, but also such fish as deep-water sharks
LIFE SPAN	Up to 23 years

ANIMAL FACTS

These seals have a highly efficient *respiratory* (breathing) system, which enables them to dive for up to two hours without surfacing for air. During the breeding season, bulls stake a claim to their breeding *territories* (home areas). Then pregnant females arrive, giving birth soon afterward. The pups are weaned relatively quickly and must then fend for themselves. The females mate again before returning to the sea.

Killer whales represent the only major threat to adult southern elephant seals.

Males of this species are the largest of all seals, weighing as much as 8,800 pounds (4,000 kilograms). Southern elephant seals also dive deeper than other seals, to about 5,250 feet (1,600 meters).

WHERE IN THE WORLD?

Found in the Southern Ocean around Antarctica.

SWIMMING
Elephant seals swim with their hind flippers. They undertake two major migrations each year in search of food, the second lasting up to eight months.

MOUTH
This appears very red, sometimes creating the impression of bleeding.

HEAD SHAPE
The massive, trunklike structure on the head of the males explains their common name.

COLORATION
Both sexes are dark gray, slightly lighter in color on the underparts.

PROTECTION
A thick layer of *blubber* (fat) lies under the skin. This fat provides insulation and serves as a reserve of food.

HOW BIG IS IT?

MOTHER AND PUP
Females and offspring live together on land only until the pups are weaned. Nearly half of all pups do not survive their first year at sea.

Northern Fur Seal

VITAL STATISTICS

WEIGHT	65–600 lb (30–275 kg); males are heavier than females
LENGTH	4.6–6.9 ft (1.4–2.1 m)
SEXUAL MATURITY	Females 3–5 years; males 5–6 years, but rarely mate before 10
LENGTH OF PREGNANCY	248 days; development starts about 4 months after mating
NUMBER OF OFFSPRING	1; weaning occurs at 26 weeks
DIET	Hunts a variety of fish and squid
LIFE SPAN	Males up to 17 years; females up to 26 years

ANIMAL FACTS

Northern fur seals spend most of their life in the ocean, returning to land only to breed. At this stage, the males—called bulls—will not feed for up to two months as they battle to control mating *territories* (personal areas). Females are attracted to males with the best territories. Dominant bulls may establish harems numbering up to 50 cows. The dense underfur of this species consists of 350,000 individual hairs per square inch (60,000 per square centimeter).

Females have a significantly longer life span than males.

Northern fur seals were hunted extensively for their pelts until the practice was banned in 1996. Their numbers continue to fall, possibly because of overfishing of their prey.

WHERE IN THE WORLD?

Found in the northern Pacific Ocean. Its main breeding areas, called rookeries, are on the Commander Pribilof and Tyuleni islands in the Bering Sea.

FACE
Both sexes have a short muzzle, with the nose extending beyond the jaws in bulls.

WHISKERS
Whiskers are very long—white in adults but black in youngsters.

MALE PHYSIQUE
Males have a thick, wide, powerful neck with a mane of longer, coarser guard hairs.

FLIPPERS
Fur seals can rotate their hind flippers forward and down to walk on land. They swim using only their front flippers.

HOW BIG IS IT?

FIGHTING
Males seeking to control a mating territory try first to intimidate any rivals. If fighting follows, males can bite using their long, sharp *canine* (tearing) teeth.

Walrus

VITAL STATISTICS

WEIGHT	2,750–3,000 lb (1,250–1,400 kg); males are heavier than females
LENGTH	8–12 ft (2.4–3.5 m); up to 5 ft (1.5 m) tall
SEXUAL MATURITY	6–7 years; males rarely mate before 15
LENGTH OF PREGNANCY	365 days; development starts 3–4 months after mating
NUMBER OF OFFSPRING	1; weaning occurs at 26 weeks
DIET	Hunts shellfish, fish, and octopus; occasionally kills seals and scavenges on whale remains
LIFE SPAN	40 years

ANIMAL FACTS

Male walruses, called bulls, battle ferociously on land during the breeding period. They can inflict serious injuries with their tusks, but the largest males usually intimidate other individuals. In the sea, walruses can dive to depths of 250 feet (75 meters) in search of food, relying on their whiskers to locate prey on the seabed. Walruses face few dangers, though they are at risk from killer whales and polar bears.

These massive seals are unmistakable. They are the only seal with tusks. Their distinctive long tusks—actually modified teeth—are present in both sexes.

WHERE IN THE WORLD?

Lives in the Pacific, off Alaska and in the Chukchi Sea. Atlantic population extends from northern Canada to Greenland. Both populations move south in winter.

BLUBBER
Fat reaching up to 6 inches (15 centimeters) thick beneath the skin protects them against the cold.

WHISKERS
Up to 700 whiskers are arranged in 15 rows.

FLIPPERS
The flippers are smooth and free of hair on their upper surface.

TUSKS
Male tusks can measure 36 inches (90 centimeters) long, but female tusks are shorter.

MOBILITY
Walruses need to be able to leave the sea and haul themselves onto land.

GAINING A HOLD
The front flippers act as anchors, helping to pull the body up.

HAULING OUT
The walrus then uses its tusks to help pull itself onto land.

FLOATING ALONG
During the winter and spring, walruses drift on large *ice floes* (chunks of ice).

HOW BIG IS IT?

Harp Seal

SPECIES • *Pagophilus groenlandicus*

The harp-shaped pattern on the adult's back explains the common name of these seals. People have long hunted the young pups for their valuable fur, though this practice has become controversial.

VITAL STATISTICS

WEIGHT	400 lb (180 kg)
LENGTH	5.25–6.25 ft (1.6–1.9 m)
SEXUAL MATURITY	Females 4–6 years; males 5–6 years
LENGTH OF PREGNANCY	About 225 days; development starts about 4.5 months after fertilization
NUMBER OF OFFSPRING	1; weaning occurs by 12 days
DIET	Feeds on a variety of fish, including capelin, cod, and herring, also crabs and squid
LIFE SPAN	30–35 years

WHERE IN THE WORLD?

Lives in the Arctic and northwestern Atlantic, breeding in the Gulf of St. Lawrence off Newfoundland, east of Greenland, and in the White Sea.

ANIMAL FACTS

Harp seals spend most of the year in the ocean. They only return to the sea ice to give birth. During this period, they gather in dense groups. They are then vulnerable to being hunted by polar bears. Young harp seals are pale yellow at birth, but by three days old their coat will have become snowy white. The pups grow very quickly, tripling their birth weight of 24 pounds (11 kilograms) before they are weaned.

PATTERNING
Adults have a black head, in addition to the harp-shaped marking on the back. Their fur is otherwise pale gray.

EARLESS SEALS
Harp seals are considered "earless" because they do not have flaps covering the openings of their ears. Nevertheless, they have excellent hearing on land and in the water.

HIND FLIPPERS
These move from side to side to push the harp seal through the water.

COLORATION
The darker areas of fur are slightly lighter in females than in males.

FRONT FLIPPERS
These tend to look more like paws than flippers.

ON THE MOVE
Harp seals and other earless seals use their hind flippers to swim (far right). Sea lions and other seals with earflaps (right) use their front flippers to swim.

HOW BIG IS IT?

Females nurse their young for only about 10 minutes every four hours or so. Otherwise, the pups are left alone.

Gray Whale

VITAL STATISTICS

WEIGHT	30–40 tons (27.2–36.3 metric tons); females are slightly bigger than males
LENGTH	23–43 ft (7–13 m)
SEXUAL MATURITY	5–11 years
LENGTH OF PREGNANCY	365–400 days
NUMBER OF OFFSPRING	1; weaning occurs after 7–8 months
DIET	Filter-feeders, sucking up *crustaceans* (shelled animals with jointed legs), as well as worms on the sea floor
LIFE SPAN	Over 80 years

Gray whales undertake one of the longest migrations of any creature on Earth, from the Arctic to waters off Mexico. They are too large for predators to attack, though killer whales hunt newborn whales.

WHERE IN THE WORLD?

Lives in the eastern North Pacific Ocean, in the Bering and Chukchi seas, migrating each October to their breeding lagoons in Baja California.

ANIMAL FACTS

These whales swim up to 14,000 miles (22,530 kilometers) when migrating to and from their breeding grounds. Instead of teeth, they have thin plates called baleen. They use the plates to filter tiny animals from the mud, sand, and water they suck into their mouths. They feed mainly on small, shrimplike creatures called krill. People nearly hunted gray whales into extinction in the 1800's and early 1900's. Their numbers have recovered significantly since protection of the species began in 1947.

The underlying gray coloration of these whales is not always obvious.

BARNACLES
Some of the white blotches on a gray whale's skin are barnacles, shelled ocean animals that attach themselves to a hard surface for their adult life.

DORSAL SWELLING
A prominent *dorsal* (back) hump is present here, but there is no actual fin.

TAIL FINS
The flukes have pointed tips and are up to 12 feet (3.7 meters) wide.

WHALE LICE
Large groups of these parasites, which appear as yellow patches, feed on whale skin and damaged tissue.

BREACHING
A gray whale may rise from the water and fall back with a huge splash. It may do this to communicate with other whales, or to knock whale lice off its body, or just for fun. Scientists are not sure why.

HOW BIG IS IT?

Narwhal

VITAL STATISTICS

WEIGHT	Up to 3.5 tons (3.2 metric tons); males are much bigger than females
LENGTH	13–15 ft (4–4.6 m)
SEXUAL MATURITY	Females 4–7 years; males 8–9 years
LENGTH OF PREGNANCY	Around 465 days; calves are brown at birth
NUMBER OF OFFSPRING	1; weaning may take 2 years
DIET	Includes such fish as Arctic cod, plus squid, octopus, and shrimplike animals
LIFE SPAN	Up to 50 years

The tusks of male narwhals were once sold as "horns" from a mythical beast known as a unicorn. Some people paid small fortunes for these tusks, believing they could prevent death.

WHERE IN THE WORLD?

Found in the far north, in eastern Canada and around much of the coast of Greenland, extending across the Arctic north of Europe and Asia.

ANIMAL FACTS

The narwhal's unusual tusk is actually an elongated tooth that grows out of the left side of its upper jaw. It can reach nearly 9 feet (2.7 centimeters) in length. The tusk is probably used to attract mates. It also helps the narwhal to sense water temperature and pressure. Narwhals live in small groups, but they sometimes gather in clusters of several thousand. Their unusual name means *corpse whale,* referring to their gray coloration and the way they often swim upside down like a dead animal.

Narwhal tusks are made of ivory, like the tusks of an elephant.

RIDGE
There is no *dorsal* (back) fin in these whales, but a ridge extends down the middle of the back.

APPEARANCE
Heavily mottled on the upperparts of the body, these whales are paler on the flanks and underside. Old males become mainly white.

FLIPPERS
These are relatively short and broad.

SAY THE NAME
The name *narwhal* is pronounced *NAHR hwuhl.*

TUSK
Only males have long, tightly spiralled tusks, though some females have short tusks.

DANGEROUS LIVING
Narwhals may fall victim to attacks by killer whales. They also sometimes drown after becoming trapped under the ice.

HOW BIG IS IT?

Beluga Whale

VITAL STATISTICS

WEIGHT	1,984–3,306 lb (900–1,500 kg); males are bigger than females
LENGTH	12–18 ft (3.5–5.5 m)
SEXUAL MATURITY	Females 5 years; males 8 years
LENGTH OF PREGNANCY	Around 465 days
NUMBER OF OFFSPRING	1; weaning may last for 2 years
DIET	Fish such as capelin, salmon, Arctic char and cod, as well as squid, octopus, and marine worms
LIFE SPAN	Over 50 years

Beluga whales possess a remarkable ability to find open stretches of water in the Arctic sea ice, enabling them to surface and breathe in this forbidding environment.

WHERE IN THE WORLD?

Lives throughout the Arctic Ocean, though it is most common in shallow waters, extending as far south as Hudson Bay in Canada.

ANIMAL FACTS

Belugas are smaller than most other whales. They are sometimes called sea canaries, because they make a variety of high-pitched sounds. Some of these sounds are clicks. The whales use the echoes of clicks to sense their surroundings, an ability called echo-location. Other sounds are used for commun-ication. Belugas are highly social animals. They live in groups called pods, which are usually made up of about a dozen individuals. However, belugas sometimes gather in groups of several thousand.

The hard tissue on the beluga's head, called the "melon," is used to make and hear sounds.

NECK STRUCTURE
The bones of the neck are not joined, allowing belugas to turn their heads from side to side.

COLORATION
Adults turn white at around seven to nine years. Females change earlier than males do.

BACK
There is no *dorsal* (back) fin. The beluga's generic name, *Delphinapterus* means *dolphin without a fin*.

YOUNG
Young belugas are gray or brown at birth but soon become bluish-gray.

HUNTING
Polar bears are a significant danger to belugas, especially to young calves. The bears seize belugas when they surface for air.

HOW BIG IS IT?

Emperor Penguin

VITAL STATISTICS

WEIGHT	66–100 lb (30–45 kg)
HEIGHT	Up to 4 ft (1.2 m)
SEXUAL MATURITY	Females 5 years; males 5–6 years
NUMBER OF EGGS	1
INCUBATION PERIOD	63 days; exposure to the freezing air can be fatal; young form groups called creches, and head to sea at about 3 months old, when the pack ice breaks up in spring
DIET	Fish, shrimplike animals, and squid
LIFE SPAN	15–20 years

ANIMAL FACTS

Emperor penguins travel up to 62 miles (100 kilometers) to their breeding colonies in Antarctica. The hen then lays a single egg, which she passes to her mate. She returns to the sea to feed. He carries the egg on his feet, insulated by a roll of skin. Males huddle together through the dark, treacherous Antarctic winter. They face winds of 112 miles (180 kilometers) per hour and temperatures as low as –80 °F (–62 °C). They take turns on the outside of the huddle, where conditions are worst. The males do not eat for nine weeks, until their partners return. The two parents then alternate trips to the sea to feed and bring back food for the newly hatched chick.

These are the largest of all penguins. They are the only large animal to spend the winter on the surface of Antarctica. Emperor penguins must work together to survive under such incredibly harsh conditions.

WHERE IN THE WORLD?

Lives off the coast of Antarctica, traveling inland to breed.

APPEARANCE
Yellow areas on each side of the head become paler and merge over the breast.

PLUMAGE
This is dense, with up to 70 feathers per square inch (10.85 per square centimeter) of body surface, making it highly effective at trapping body heat.

WINGS
These are used as flippers, which penguins flap to move through the water. Although penguins are birds, they cannot fly.

CHICKS
Chicks have black and white patterning on their head and a dense gray down coat.

SHARED PARENTING
After transferring the egg, the hen goes off to feed. When the male later hands back the chick, he may have lost one-third of his body weight.

DIVING DEEP

Emperor penguins dive deeper than any other bird—down to 1,850 feet (565 meters). They can stay underwater for nearly 20 minutes.

HOW BIG IS IT?

Glossary

adaptation a characteristic of an organism that makes it better able to survive and reproduce in its environment

alpine high elevations, especially on mountains, beyond which trees will not grow because of the cold

amphibian an animal with scaleless skin that usually lives part of its life in water and part on land

baleen thin, horny plates growing downward from the upper jaws or palates of certain whales

barnacle the only crustacean that stays in one position during its adult life

blubber a thick layer of fat that lies under the skin and over the muscles of whales, dolphins, porpoises, seals, sea cows, and other sea mammals that protects the animals from cold

breaching the action of a whale in leaping free of the surface of the ocean and falling back with a huge splash

burrow underground shelter

canine a long, pointed tooth near the front of the mouth used for tearing

cloud forests dense forests in tropical areas that are almost constantly covered by clouds

cloven hoof a hoof divided into an even number of toes, usually two

crustacean an invertebrate with many jointed legs and a hard external shell, including lobsters and shrimp

dewclaw an often-useless extra claw or toe found on some hoofed mammals

domesticate to change an animal or plant from a wild to a tame state suitable for agriculture

dorsal on or near the back

echolocation a system in which animals use the echoes of sounds they produce to collect information about their surroundings

habitat the kind of place in which an animal lives

hibernation an inactive, sleeplike state that some animals enter during the winter

ice floe a large floating chunk of ice

ice shelf a ledge of ice sticking out into the sea from an ice sheet

incisor a tooth having a sharp edge for cutting

incubate to keep fertilized eggs and young animals under proper conditions for growth and development

invertebrate an animal without a backbone

krill small, shrimplike animals that live in oceans throughout the world

lichen any of a group of living things that consist of a fungus and a simple organism growing together in a single unit

mammal an animal that feeds its young on the mother's milk

melon the hard tissue on the beluga's head used to make and hear sounds

molar a tooth with a broad surface for grinding

parasite a living thing that feeds off another living thing called a host

pod a small group of whales or seals

predator an animal that preys upon other animals

reverse migration a movement into areas with harsh weather, often to avoid predators

rookery a breeding place or colony where other birds or animals are crowded together

species a group of animals or plants that have certain permanent characteristics in common and are able to interbreed

subspecies a subdivision of a species

talon the claw of an animal, especially a bird of prey

territory an area within definite boundaries, such as a nesting ground, in which an animal lives and from which it keeps out others of its kind

thermal a rising current of warm air

venom a poisonous substance produced by many kinds of animals to injure, kill, or digest prey

wean to accustom a young animal to food other than its mother's milk

Resources

Books

Alpine Tundra: Life on the Tallest Mountain by
Salvatore Tocci (Franklin Watts, 2005)
Learn about the animals, plants, climate, and
people that live in the alpine tundra environment.

Journey into the Arctic by Bryan Alexander and
Cherry Alexander (Oxford University Press, 2003)
This volume paints a picture of the lives of both
Arctic animals and Arctic-dwelling people.

Mountains by Seymour Simon (Mulberry Books,1997)
This classic volume is filled with photographs and
vivid text describing the characteristics and
ecology of our planet's mountains.

*Poles Apart: Why Penguins and Polar Bears
Will Never Be Neighbors* by Elaine Scott (Viking, 2004)
Award-winning science writer Elaine Scott describes the
similarities and differences between the polar regions.

Websites

Antarctica: The End of the Earth
http://www.pbs.org/wnet/nature/antarctica/index.html
This interactive website from PBS takes a fascinating look
at the animals who survive and even thrive in the extremes
of the Antarctic region.

BBC Nature: Mountains
http://www.bbc.co.uk/nature/habitats/Mountain
At this site, videos take visitors into beautiful mountain
ranges around the world, from the Alps to the Himalaya
and beyond.

WWF Global: Ecoregions
http://wwf.panda.org/about_our_earth/ecoregions/
about/habitat_types/habitats/
Explore the ecology of mountain and polar regions at this
website from the World Wide Fund for Nature (WWF).

Acknowledgments

Cover photograph: Photo Researchers (J.-L. Klein and
M.-L. Hubert)

Illustrations: © Art-Tech; Stanley W. Galli, WORLD BOOK

Photographs:

Alexandre Buisse: 15

Corbis RF: 22

Dreamstime: 8 (M. Blajenov), 12 (U. Ravbar), 20 (C. Lips),
25 (H. Leyrer), 33 (L. Christiansen), 37 (A. Hathaway)

FLPA: 6 (D. Hosking), 14 (K. Wothe), 23 (R. Tidman),
24 (S. Huwiler), 28 (M. Durham), 29 (D. Middleton),
35 (T. Sbampato), 42 (F. Nicklin), 43 (F. Nicklin)

iStock Photo: 11 (Stephen Forster)

NOAA: 39 (Budd Christman), 40 (Budd Christman)

Photos.com: 9, 10, 13, 18, 19, 21, 26, 27, 30, 31, 32, 33, 34,
38, 41, 44, 45

Science Photo Library: 17 (W. K. Fletcher)

Stock.Xchng: 7 (R. J. Leonard)

SuperStock: 16 (Tier und Naturfotografie),
36 (imagebroker)

Index